Contents.

Chapter One – HOME

Chapter Two – SELF

Chapter Three – LOVE

We made killing ourselves enjoyable & addictive.

HOME

It's within the madness that we can find some peace.

the proof is in the pudding

I plant my feet in the
tall
green
grass

To feel rooted

To leave an imprint

If only for a moment

Some proof

that I was here.

red and yellow

Red & yellow brick townhouses
Three or four in a row.
Over the road from the
oppressively grey painted council flats.
One of those streets that everybody knows

Weather battered
Rubbish littered
Tarmac punished
People bitter

You can see it's been forgotten.

Hidden in plain sight,
A kind of maze-like system
A peculiar little place,
full of dead ends, alleyways
and alcoholism.

A labyrinth you'd avoid at night,
rather go home the long way,
because I've watched the junkies
looking to score
and still somehow fail to navigate.

That shop was held up with an axe.
That school once burned down.
As dangerous as this city's river.
If you enter
you'll probably drown

But today, I'm just cutting through
Avoiding the mid-day traffic.
Windows up and doors locked,
maybe paranoid and a little erratic.

code

Dots and dashes
Lines never whole
Starved of your soul
My incomplete

Lines of ashes
To pay the toll
Bestowed control
Rests at my feet

night fall

The night creeps in
and slips its hands
over my skin
and covers my eyes.

Suffocating.

This cold cracked spine
can only do its best,
and on my thoughts
the darkness dines.
Pitch black,
expressionless.

Descending

Sinking deeper

Slipping away

Another dreamless slumber.
Unstoppable and never ending
again.

above & beyond

Back lit,
black canopy
hanging overhead.
Something vast
and ever expanding,
looking down.

Then there's me.

A speck of dust
nothing more,
just stood
looking up,
my feet too firm
upon the ground.

reach don't touch

As time fails me,
I search for the answers
through the thickets
of my thoughts.

I expected so much more.

And so,   I wait.

I can see what is real,
though I'm unable to touch.
I can see into the distance,
but whenever I reach
It's never
          quite
                    far
                              enough.

if you can't see it, it can't hurt you
(Regional Dialect)

I distance ma'self from what might die,
in an attempt to separate ma'self from feeling.
Collecting missed opportunities,
like loose change found down't back o't sofa.
        Unknowingly discarded.
As the once vibrant lives lose worth

        and lose meaning.

And so't bloodline ends.
Nowt but a memory,
until it's fully forgotten.
Through stupor or sickness?

Over time ya can remove't choice to actually ***be*** better.
I know this, cos I've seen it.

Ya can kill ya'self without actually dying.
Dramatically change, yet remain't same.

With all o' this in mind,
sometimes ma lungs feel so 'eavy
wit burden o' breathing,

For a moments respite

I just stop.

if you can't see it, it can't hurt you

I distance myself from what might die,
in an attempt to separate myself from feeling.
Collecting missed opportunities,
like loose change found down
the back of the sofa,
        Unknowingly discarded.
As those once vibrant lives lose worth

       and lose meaning.

And so the bloodline ends.
Nothing but a memory,
until it's fully forgotten.
Through stupor or sickness?

Over time you can remove the choice
to actually *be* better
I know this
Because I've seen it

You can kill yourself without actually dying.
Dramatically change, yet remain the same.

With all of this in mind,
sometimes my lungs feel so heavy
with the burden of breathing,

For a moments respite

I just stop.

piano

Each tender key played; I can always feel.
Closing my heavy eyes to understand.
Having such sight without the need to see,
the ivory becomes one with the hand.
A thing of beauty can be so haunting,
something that leaves no space for any doubt.
Overwhelming yet never so daunting.
Filling my lungs with an urge to scream out,
letting the sweetness take over it all.
Leaving me stranded in a breathless state
with an undeniable need for more,
yet this divinity often comes late.
And I am left only to wonder when?
Until it does come, I'm left to pretend.

small boy

soft teeth
hard bite
lock jaw
aggressor

fists clenched
fear builds
tears stream
throughout

small boy
big dreams
too weak
frozen

my eyes fill with pain
for her

white knuckles
stiff palm
screaming
cowering

waiting for a war to pass us by
for the dark clouds to dissipate

thirty-year-old bruises
is that how long they last?

discoloured memories   they fade

but never go away

and it's gone

Lost with time is something nobody can regain
Birthed behind sight, in childhood.
Wrapped in cotton wool
and the most delicate glass.
A sickly-sweet song
O the naivety plagues our bones the same.

> Innocence
> > Something that once was
> Now gone

finders' keepers

You wanted me to need you.
You wanted me to be dependent.
Something I eventually saw
with hindsight.

You kept me as the kid that looked up to you,
until I found purpose with someone new.
I was stepping out of your shadow
and into the light.

I finally found myself when I lost you.

i, the enemy

With little option,
a harbinger of ending
carries me.

The aura of malaise,
with an immersive approach
                                    to living.

That familiar feeling,
capitulation.
To you I'm giving.

Surrender
is my act of defiance.

I sing your name with a bitter tongue.

I sign myself away with blood.

frames & acres

They can tear me down,
burn me alive
to reveal this ivory framework.

They'll gather for the fall,
to feast on all of my failures.
Hovering in their swarms,
the casket ready and tailored.

See this heart, it's caged, entombed,
It's held in nobody's favour.
Scorched through blackened bone.
Alone.
Abandoned in empty acres.

ORBIT

My Mother
 The sun

My father
 The moon

I dread the darkness to come.

*I would rather keep searching in the dark
with the possibility of finding something new
than constantly treading light whilst pretending
to be whole.*

SELF

Amongst the crowds
I'm faceless
Nameless

Not even a
number.

tidal

There's a siren singing inside my head,
Parting crashing waves of thoughts, do I drown?
A never-ending flow of something more,
I am one with the sunken ships, let down.
Submerging beneath the words lesser said,
Wishing the minutes away with no sound.
The water creeps in, I ask what is left?
A wreck on the ocean floor, never found.
I held on so long now I'm out of breath,
Thoughts wash upon the shore to stare at clouds.

the willow tree

Sat beneath a willow tree,
Skin bare in sweltering heat
To reveal what could be described as
a "dad bod". (Though I'm not a father)

Between the haze & breeze,
I'm reading poetry of perceived masculinity;
In a world that demands
A man to be manly, strong and never cry.
                              (We can never cry)
A woman to be feminine
yet ooze power & strength.
            (But also, be soft, silky smooth and sensual)

And I think to myself
            You don't need to be a hooker
            to make sex sell,
            but you can still be a whore.

So how are we to know
just what we're supposed to be?
Avenues and alleyways aplenty
Signposts bring us full circle.
We yearn for more, constantly
and we always feel oh so empty.

How can we truly define, when we question
the most basic of things?
Everything we think we see.
Everything we think we are.

It's just another thought
that eventually comes to pass.
She walks on over to seal it shut with a kiss.
The end of a thought
beneath the willow tree.

naivety

I was once a boy that thought he was the man.
There's a certain arrogance in youth.

It's an acquired taste.

multiple personality

It's hard to just be me,
when I feel like
a *million* different people.

the orchestra

I am a thousand songs
all playing at once.
Singing in chaotic harmony

My heart, the metronome,
Keeping time.
A constant beat.

Love

        Hate

Triumph

        Defeat

        Eventually the music will fade.

something hurt

Every addict in me
scratches and screams to get out.

Out from under pressures and the restraint
of a world that keeps me down.

> The sunny side of life
> tries to keep me in check
> telling me to put on a smile.

I can't...

Behind closed doors,
caged like an animal.
It's something that I try to hide

> Especially from myself.

rebel?

> Every now and then
> I burn an effigy of myself
> in an act
> of self-defiance.

sense

I find myself bare,
steeped in the sound
of intermittent innocence.

Stripped back
to the bone and sinew,
a kind of comforting dissonance.

Like the air around me
                                 Clings

It holds

         It breaks apart   what was

Now my lungs reject the need to breath.
My open eyes refuse to see.
I hear
        but I can't accept.

You sung away my senses,
leaving this heart
unable to feel.
Leaving me completely inept.

fractions

Today
one-quarter of my heart has gone away
leaving me three quarters sombre,
with a tear that hangs
from the corner of my eye.

Temporary though it may be,
I feel the dullest of aches
that vibrates within my bones

Is this love?

play it safe

If heaven is real then call me a fool
but until I know I'm playing it cool.

God ain't got nothing on me
and the devil's songs are too sweet.

Head down on my knees
I'm just praying for the irony
that when the angel of mercy
chooses to show,
she'll turn her back
yet I'll never know.

I'm taking it all back
Just pull me from the quick sand
I'M TAKING IT BACK!
I'm going to the promised land
I'M TAKING IT BACK!
With my demons, hand in hand

They won't take me back
SOMEBODY PRAY FOR ME!
They won't take me back
ONCE I WAS BLIND
BUT NOW I SEE

Without any answers
there are still a million questions.
So, if heaven smells like freedom
You've got to question
what you've been breathing.

tempting as it may be

The devils hand
weighs heavy upon my shoulder.
Ice cold breath
on the back of my neck,
chilling me to the core.

To be honest
I see the appeal
Anarchy
Chaos

The appeal of something else

A revolution against man.
A revolution against god.

men!

I see men younger than me
always trying to be older.
Dressed to impress
in designer gear,
each day
trying to be bolder.

Peacocking

I see men younger than me,
settled into older ways.
The routine of sinking jars
with a game of darts
until last orders are called,
every night the same
at the local bar.

Stagnant

I see men younger than me,
pretending to be older.
Seeing life as a race,
I don't understand such haste
or the maturity being faked.
I just let them brush past my shoulders

is this enough?

I begin to gather myself.
Trying to figure out
where everything goes,
by looking at the spaces
left by the missing pieces.

Shards scattered across a floor.

But please tell me…
Do they have to fit perfectly?

Because all that was lost
may never be found

Not in its entirety

What's left, can it be refashioned?

There's never a definitive answer.

For now, I'll just wait
and fill any gaps
with dust and sound.

LOVE

Nothing good comes
from clinging on to thorns.

How can we miss what we never had?
Why can't we let go of what's gone?

my *sugar sickness*

Wrap my starved body
in the silken palms of your hands,
      Tight!
I succumb to something hidden
      and I'll never understand.

Words that cannot be spoken aloud,
yet they scream
with each passing glance.

      Longing for that taste of sweetness.

Like sugar that is stuck
upon the tip of my tongue,
It's there that your name hangs back.
Hiding behind my teeth,
waiting to come undone.

I bite down hard
to hold on,
please stay.
Clinging to each passing moment
before they begin fade.

cove

Broken
scarred earth.
A land bound mass
built by time.
Traced with dry cracked brick walls,
Soaking in a sea of green.

Aged
stone flesh.
A face weathered
by time,
twelve or so thousand years more
than you and I.

Captured by each sunrise
Released with every sunset,
yet always guarded
by the sky.

And every cloud that passes
is but a fleeting romance.

makes sense to me

To know that I have loved,
fills me with something
more than joy.
Beyond elation.
>   *I'd let you break my heart.*

question everything

I see clearly
Pain
Destruction
Struggle

And I ask myself
"Am I the change you need to make"

no smokers allowed

You were just another lesson
that I had to learn.

I exhale you like cigarette smoke
with a thankful sigh.
>   Relieved.

I'm glad I don't smoke anymore.

just like a dream makes sense?

Eyes like an ocean
Such perilous waters heed warning
But something haunts me

A question

I wonder how many have died at sea?

    I'm here on a makeshift raft, waiting.

        You were there again
        Tempting the night sky
        And as the sun sank beneath the crashing waves
        I exhaled a resting sigh.

    You're ready to pull me under

    Paralysed, I cannot fight this ten-ton slumber

    We passed on a bridge as strangers
    but with some recognition;
    Something familiar.
    Some kind of Déjà vu.
    I just know that there is truth
    to this life stranger than fiction.

open invitation

You take your clothes off,
an open invitation
to feel love.
Never a shadow of doubt
or responsibility.

You mastered the art
of separation
from yourself,
during a lover's drought.
An offering of flesh
so willingly.

I cut myself
from the picture
and burned a hole
straight through this love,
to separate myself
from you
and this melody.

5ive thoughts

1)
I can feel you
clawing
Pulling my ribs apart
in search of answers.
Wanting
Grasping in the dark
and only finding more questions.

                    2)
                    It left my heart bruised
                    I knew it wasn't love
                    only infatuation
                              I couldn't give up
                              the pain.

3)
I refuse to carry the guilt
that you so wrongly gifted.

                    4)
                    knife by knife
                    I pull you from my back.

5)
I try to forget the past
I turn you into
a blurred image
Distorted
        A ghost

To me, now   you were never really there.

pocket fluff

Come find me with
the missing pieces,
tangled up
in thread and lint.
Taking all I can.
Taking whatever comes to mind

Fingers no longer wrapped,
but once they were.
Just like intertwining vines.

Skinned knuckles
with a calloused fist full of air,
that's heavy with frustration.
       Inside,
that's where we used to be.
Stealing moments and biding time
with no fear of temptation.

memories edge

You kissed my wrist
      delicately
in an attempt
to make me feel.

The purge is always
a by-product of hurt.

lost cause paradox
With a heavy heart, I hold you close,
these arms stretched out, aching to help
      …but I can't.

XYLOPHONE

no matter how hard I tried
i could never fill the void

now i'm nothing
but a fading chimed echo
that bounces between
your ribs.

exit wound

I can only compare you
to being shot.

The impact was heavy.
You pierced me.
Breaking the surface,
getting under my skin.
Deep
beneath the flesh.

When you left,
you took a part of me.
Leaving - something - missing.
Damage.

I can only compare you
to being shot.

RISE

Honesty is a dying art

hush your mouth

They put a bounty on the head,
an open promise of bloodshed
for anyone that speaks
a word of worth.

They tell you
that you're free
to think and to speak,
until they don't like the words.

They need to keep you in check.
A ready rope for your neck.
A knife behind their back
that you can't see.

They need to keep you on your knees
unable to see
with mouths open wide,
so you can eat up the lies
that they have to feed.

THE PRIVILEGED FAVOUR THE PRIVILEGED

you know who you are!

The ones who think
that they're the elite

A cut above the rest

Believe me when I say
    You're nothing to me

You are what's wrong
Not everybody else

No title will change that!

heavy weight

The spine that is crooked
cannot handle pressure
and will surely crumble.
    Time exposes **all**.

£conomically viable

To the ones who rest upon thrones.

We do exist!
(and *they do know)*

And though we are named
                              to most.

To them

We are but numbers

No personality

No features

No true identity

Faceless
Nameless

Just a tally of
living, dead or dying;
alongside our economic value
on a spreadsheet.

What do you bring to the table?

It costs **them** more to "*keep*" us.
So begs the question…
What is *your* worth to the keepers?

metaphor (June 2020)

a glass sits under a dripping tap for days
(the water pleading for freedom)
slowly
surely
undoubtedly
filling
cold stainless-steel surrounding
(the environment always says to stay in your place)
empty
hard
suppressive
reflecting
filling mil by mil
day by day
until it finally reaches the brim
slowly
surely
obviously
naturally
the water starts to spill over the edge
free from being contained
only to realise
it broke free into a larger cage
and the work must start again.

in my humble opinion

It seems that nowadays you have to scream to be heard and
strip to be seen;
selling your soul to the masses as if *likes* were currency.
Nowadays, we only follow the leaders, the pioneers of the
filtered regime;
governments have nothing to offer.
Hell no.
Not for me.
They have let us down too many times.
Nowadays, we want to exist inside a bubble of apparent
reality with our lives available on screens.
We want money, sex, life, and death and don't forget that
we **need** celebrity.
This is what makes us whole nowadays.

Nowadays, we feed from digital interaction,
an abundance of misinformation,
and misguided attraction.
Nothing is real,
this is our everything,
our new religion,
and we're offended by everything.

endless

Some days
positivity is hard to muster.
Some days
you have to dig to find it.

Never stop digging!

The trenches may run deep
but it's so worthwhile.

With every new day,
the possibilities are endless.

another celebrity?

Wake up early, pour some coffee, put my glasses on, and turn on the TV. I flick to the news to see what's occurring as I release a wide-mouthed yawn. It must have been a slow day. Either that or they're just bored of famine, death, and decay.
Instead, I'm force-fed celebrity,
filled with arrogance and dressed as deities. I think to myself:
> *"Is this it? Does this actually matter?"*
The rich doing their bit dressed up in Gucci and Prada; tongues wag and jaws drop to the floor when they see such sights.
I understand the need to escape living vicariously in this hollow way but it keeps the wrong things in the light and things now need to change.
For minds to form and take real shape, there can be no more false idols full of self-importance and induced by fame.
One day, I hope to see more than who has the biggest diamond ring or who's wearing what this eve.
I want people to feel free, not trapped by a fake life.
I want to see the world beginning to heal with immediate effect. For this generation and the next to deny fake heroes saying, *"We do not accept."*
There is still time to make a difference in our minds on equality in gender, sexuality, and race. With enough money to end famine and poverty and let the young truly dream.

No more false idols.

And please, no more celebrity.

don't believe the hype

Blood on the streets
is nothing new

We're just distracted
on a regular basis.

What you
See
Hear
Read
Believe
All depends on you.

it's all about perception

Your perception of reality
is this just that

Your perception.

Life is open to interpretation.

vital

I need a breakdown
breakthrough
a life in layers, strewn
paralysis
across the floor.

Brain dead
static feed
animalistic
hate breeds
intentions of deception
leaving us battered
and begging for more.

But what do I know
about hope and broken bones?
When this hope is just a
lie sold to fools and now
chaos is vital for the cause.

Every damned day
all of your colours
turn to grey
but the superficial heroes
still crave the applause.

HAS THE WORLD EVER NOT BEEN ON FIRE?

bricks

The brittle bricks
you use to build all foundations,
to then be stacked
high & heavy
with burden & mistrust.
Bound together
with trick knot rope,
yet you want things to stand true,
demanding that it's a MUST!

The slightest bit of bad weather
leads what you've built to falter.
Your house of cards at risk of tumble
as the rebellious rain beats down
causing all faux things to crumble.

Brick by brick

An empty promise laid upon a broken wish
and just for fun, sealed with a sarcastic kiss.
Every toc to the next tic
reveals each & every opportunity
that you missed
to get things right

You had to know that what you had built
would eventually fall down.
Each and every brick
on every broken body,
yet you never hear a sound.
The voice of reason eludes you
and your integrity sits so lonesome
in the lost and never to be found.

I know I'm not your favourite flavour

because

    I

        refuse

            to be

                sweet

                    alone.

I was raised to have an opinion
and taught to question EVERYTHING.

SELF

LESS

I wear this chain of broken promises
Like a noose around my neck.

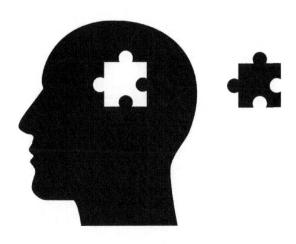

A, A & I

some days i struggle
i'm filled with regret
some days, i don't know…
i just can't help it

can't make sense
can't make me fit

i'm not a piece of
any particular puzzle
ready to be put in place
and that's that

i just don't believe that
i'm meant to fit

i have no confidence in
anything i do

so, i just stand back
let the others take their turns
let the others go first
let them take the lead
and i'll just go unseen

a life of missed opportunity
a life longing to be free
whatever that actually means

Awkward
Anxious
& Introverted
somedays it feels like a disease

surgical

i've been cut from all angles
beneath the candles
resting heavily to bird song

i've been bled by the mantle
ivy did tangle
weaving the bones for so long

left out of feeling thankful
in part dismantled
to find myself somehow gone

three more thoughts

1)
is the suture thick enough
to knit the faults together?
uneven folds test the knots.
skin too frayed to hold.

2)
i'll always be
what you need me to be

without being myself
as a whole

3)
longing for the moments
that you
are
not
here
just to give me
a little reprieve
depression

give our best

an air of sorrow
descends
leaving the world melancholic
as it harbours a sweet desolation

nothing behind those eyes
  but regret

a wretched mind
starved of fruition
intellectual malnutrition
leaving the world to wither
before the final sunset

a hint of sweetness
felt through the sour
to know thine kiss of death
o angel of mercy
and of grief
to you
we give our best

under water

i've been breaking the surface
filling my lungs with the air
that I so desperately craved

i feel better for it

but i feel like i'm slipping

the water is rising

i'm choking for breath
between being
buried by the tide
while the current
carries me away

right or rong

fragments fall
from something
once whole
they scatter
on the breeze

into the distance
into the darkness
into the void
they disappear
with ease

chase
all fingers and thumbs
a vulnerable guard
drops

it's insecurity
thinking it makes us
lesser
but we're wrong
all wrong

if i can

if i can find a solution
for every problem
for every day that passes

when the world is ending
and death comes a knocking
we can stay delusional
without a need to say

without ever stopping
we never stall
never stopping
to catch our breaths

before we all just fall

you gotta do what you gotta do

i tried to make ends meet
only to cause further distress
it just broke apart

teaching me

force should only be applied
once you've manipulated the situation
to bend in your favour

starry night

they told me there'd be brighter days
they told me to have faith & pray
now all i do is sit in the darkness
looking at the stars
trying to wish the world away

only sometimes

sometimes I feel like
i'm a rose without thorns
a shark with no teeth
a dulled down razor blade
the sun with no heat

playing possum

it's something finite
like death
but only an illusion of
being set free

from something imaginary

a dream
not reality

i see something animalistic
untamed
set free amongst
the words on a page

to ravage
to consume

now i'm awake
but still, i try to play dead

we're all just temps.

it was said that
**"holding on to anger
is like grasping a hot coal"**
and right now
my hands are blistered

stuck for words to speak
about how weighed down I feel
and how every second of my life
it seems like people are trying to steal

when the negativity
holds you by the throat - pulling down
under…
below…

gasping for air
the next breath
feels so unknown

but remember

these moments
will come to pass

because
nothing
is
permanent

everything is temporary
(yet nothing is forgotten as such)
everything is an opportunity

battle scars can build positivity

battle of self

we will never conquer
what's outside
if we do not first and foremost
overcome what resides within

LOVE part 2

The Sequel

```
The winter blows cold
I wonder where she might be
Lost in sound again
```

marrow

Love…
It's more than a word
        It's more than an emotion.

When you have it   you know!

You won't just feel it
in your heart

You'll feel it within
        the marrow of your bones.

freedom song

I trace my fingers
along the edge.
Satin skin,
so soft
but hot to the touch.

Release me.

Feel my presence.
Tongues that speak
stories of lust,
wagging in the dark.

Tell me all of your secrets
teach me how to unlock.
I'll show you all of the bones
that have laid in my closet,
hidden, for far too long.

Nails that tear
but only the surface,
as I feel you holding on.
For you my darling
I will forever bleed
a freedom song.

Release me.

Sweat soaked sin.

Release me.

proceed with caution

I was told
to only take a sip
and I knew
that they were right.

I also knew
how it would end,
but still I drank
the whole damned vial.

Poison
is what you were
to me;
And I see it now,
that lovesick misery.

I lied when I said
it was you that I need,
I just didn't care somehow.

Threw caution to the wind whilst
knowingly letting myself down.

I just wanted to know,
I wanted to feel,
how sweet you tasted
before you set me free.

I poisoned myself
with you
by choice.

north & south

There's a connection
something magnetic.
I'm drawn in with no reason,
I can't explain it.
Nor can I deny
something that is compelled
to do so.
There's just a connection.
Like forests
and endless acres.
The ocean
that soothes the beach.
Something so obvious,
like ink spilled upon paper.
Like the perfect you
and the mess of me.

4 more thoughts

1)
A rose so sweet,
so delicate.
A thing of true beauty,
still has its thorns
& I cannot tell a lie
I love it!

2)
You my dear,
are the sweetest of sins.

I betray myself
every time that I'm with you.

3)
I was just another need to fill a void.
Something to pass time.
You were counting down the seconds
until you could say goodbye.

4)
Somewhere deep
in the back of your mind,
I know you'll need me
all
over
again.

can you?

You cannot deny
a heart that bleeds.

Even from a distance,
each dying beat
still creates motion.

Like ripples in a lake
when a rock crashes the surface,
although they're now subtle

can you still feel them?

with hope

She carries the crows with her
until she is able to rest.
A sign of being ready
                    but waiting.

She conceals her cards
so close to her chest,
in memoriam.
In dedication to herself.

A swelling heart in the cavern,
waiting for an opportunity
                    to shine.

And in good health
with good wine,
the telling tongue
whispers tales of everything
and all between
life
love
loss
fear.

waste me

The scent of you lays heavy
within these once warm sheets,
where your body once rested.
I lay awake
dreaming of you.

Wrapped around me
so tight

Flesh pressing flesh

Each breath   deep

As we begin to scorch the air
around us.

Darkness fills the empty space
but we don't need to see.

I know every part of you.
You know every inch of me.

You pull me closer,
to feel all that I am.

Tear me
Break me
Feel me

Let's feed the lion to the lamb.

Leave me wasted
Leave me exhausted.

green fingers

Do you really have
any clue?

Any idea of the time spent
digging these roots?

Just trying to move you
in any way I can.

was it good for you?

I hope to god
that when you leave,
it hurts so bad

Just so I know
that what I felt
was real.

broken mirrors

Get yourself together.
Those pieces that
you thought didn't matter
well, they do!

Each and every hit
that left you broken,
that left you shattered.

They're the most important parts
of you.

Just
A
Thought

Whoever screams the loudest
gets to heaven first.

map lines

What gave us the right
to define borders and where they sit?
For the majority,
it's just the luck of the draw.
We've just got to deal with it.

Creating countries, cities, counties, towns and states
Creating divisions, inequality, ignorance and hate.

What gave us the right to say
"no sir, you can't cross this line"
and *"no madam, you can't stay here"*?

What gave us the right to instil such feelings?
When discontent for one another
becomes as easy as breathing;
As if we have some privileged, unspoken right
to pick and choose,
exerting dominance with might.

We're constantly swayed;
Advertising, social media
& governments with hidden agendas,
always fuelling hate.
Bombings, stabbings, beatings,
constantly broadcasted
until the intolerance
runs free through our veins.

Elected officials and the powers that be,
running amuck & reigning supreme.
Forever making bad decisions
and though we don't always agree,
for some reason we put up with it,
always turning the other cheek.

What gave them the right to so proudly sing?

We do!
(On a daily basis)
We close our eyes
and let them get on with it.
We think there's no other way.
We think we don't have a say.

And that's how they like it….

Ignorance is bliss
and compliance is everything.

lizard men

Society gradually becomes
crippled.
Heavy heads held
always under pressure.

Constricted constantly
Restricted repeatedly

by the serpents we call
our leaders.

hashtag NO filter

Look at this filtered life.
Eyes wider.
Teeth whiter.
It's all fake, but it's all insecurity.

Society has made you think
that there's something wrong
and there's something you need.

A "*beauty*" filter

Paying hard earned money
for a device to imply
that <u>you</u>
are not good enough.

It's a damn shame
that this is our world.
It's a crying shame
to see what we've become.

FAKE!

Ashamed to be comfortable
in our own skin,
for the fear of ridicule and judgment.
Confidence constantly crippled.
It's such a disappointment.

Now, there's nothing unique,
when being yourself is a sin.

We're all the same, look at our face.
We've all become one,
but in the worst possible way.

we

We gave everything value
and created the rich and the poor.
We created underpaid jobs
and class divisions
so we will always have to ask for more.
(But we'll say no)

We give the phones in our pockets more worth
than the sustenance that keep us alive.
We crave likes and shares
whilst ignoring cries for help
because we no longer care
about the physical and "*in 3-2-1. I'm going live*"

We've got to feed our egos.

If we can't record our good deeds,
how will we know it happened?
If we can't record our new dance,
how will we know if we're relevant?

We're taking part in a popularity contest
that's only for the best of the best,
luckily, we are.

paper thrones

For some reason it seems
that when you place yourself
on that proverbial high horse,
you lose the sight and the means
to see what others see,
or think of how they feel.

But you should remember;
The higher you put yourself,
the fall will *always* be greater.

I see favouritism on a daily basis.
I see the walls of corruption fortified
with stories and lies to try and confuse.
Any truth, they try to hide,
and then of course it's all denied.

It's every day on TV,
but also with people
that appear surround me.
It makes me sick.
The pit of my stomachs turns, it burns
with discontent and disconnect
as I try to pull away.

But what really drives me crazy
are the people that strive to be
part of that bent and spineless regime.
Thinking that they're a cut above the rest.
Thinking that they always know best.
(Even when they don't)

They'd rather pretend
and choose to defend the suited egos,
sat in their paper thrones.

in crowd

I don't want to fall
into the trap of peer pressure.
I don't want to be part
of this clique.
The elitist feel of some
will inevitably lead
to being followed by the sheep.

I see them
I see them all

I don't want to be part
of the in crowd.
I don't want to balance
on your feet.
Yet, with welcome arms
you gather them,
and with blackened eyes
they do not see.

But I see them
I see them all

I don't want to get in line.
I don't want to give my meat,
like some do so willingly.
You'd leave them starving
just so you can eat.

Feeding them on scraps of dreams,
quenching their thirst
with a false belief.
Letting them think
that you're something they need.

branded little sheep

Cover the ground in any way
that makes you happy
and lets you feel free.

Just never be cornered or *'cliqued'*
with the latest *'on trend'* disease.
Fashions are for followers,
not for the ones that lead.

Travel your own path.
Be Strong
and be grateful,
and never ever follow the sheep.

MDB
VI

The
Finale

Don't let your past be an anchor,
it's a burden you need not carry.

a proper burial

The rain beats down
on the window beside me,
as I stare
at an empty page
on a blank screen.

My eyes heavy,
my mind, over active.
I'm avoiding sleep.

Head in my hands
I listen.
Peaceful piano music
is the playlist
to this evening.

I'm giving my all
to you
and willingly
you take it.

I've uncovered the bones
of my past
so I can bury them properly,
once and for all.

When this is finally over,
you can never ask me for more.

What can any of us say
that hasn't already been said

in a million different ways,

a million times before?

Is it all just a repeat?

FIND ME ON SOCIAL MEDIA
@mdbpoetry

Thank you
for reading

Printed in Great Britain
by Amazon